AF480739

ADVANCE PRAISE FOR
THE SOURCE LADDER

"The beauty of this book is its simplicity—messages woven in a tapestry of the soul's journey and why we are here."

— Ceree Eberly, Master Akashic Records Teacher/Reader

"Ron Adams translates a deeply spiritual reality into clear, relatable understanding. His insights rekindled wisdom I had shelved for years."

— Betsy-Morgan Coffman, The Psychic Teacher

"This is one of those books that stays with you. There's a sincerity to the writing that feels real and honest, inviting reflection without ever feeling heavy."

— Ruby Miller, Certified Tarot Reader and Coach

"I got goosebumps! The ebb and flow, the remembering, the understanding, the integration — it ALL resonates."

— Wendi Boyd, Medium & Certified Tarot Master

"It read like you channeled Source."

— Audrey Siow, DC

"It's virtue is its simplicity, directness, and the awareness that shines out from these words. The distilled simplicity points to profound truth."

— Shirley Shultz Myers

THE SOURCE LADDER

The Frequencies of Being

Ronald

Copyright © 2026 The Source Ladder, LLC
Published by The Source Ladder, LLC

All rights reserved.

No part of this book may be reproduced, stored in a retrieval system,
or transmitted in any form or by any means — electronic, mechanical,
photocopying, recording, or otherwise — without prior written
permission from the author, except for brief quotations used in reviews or
scholarly work.

This book reflects the author's personal experiences and perspectives.

ISBN: 979-8-9955727-1-8

Cover and Interior Design: Rachel Sierra

First Edition

Printed in the United States of America

DEDICATION

To Source — thank you for the teachers, family, friends, acquaintances, and experiences that have made this life interesting and exciting. I look forward to whatever comes next, with a smile.

ACKNOWLEDGMENTS

Maureen
Thank you for the Akashic reading that helped set the direction for what became this book.

Ceree
Thank you for encouraging me to continue this work and for the clarity you offered along the way.

Betsy
Thank you for your support, your honesty, and your steady encouragement. Our conversations helped me stay grounded and clear as I worked through this material.

Shirley
Thank you for your structural suggestions and for taking the time to look at the manuscript with a professional eye. Your feedback helped me strengthen the organization and clarity of the book.

Lighthouse Tapestry
Thank you for welcoming me into the group and for the openness and support. I appreciate the willingness of members like Wendi and Ruby to read and respond to the manuscript.

EPIGRAPH

"I ALONE AM"
— Source

TABLE OF CONTENTS

Preface
INTRODUCTION

PART ONE — The Nature of the Seeker   1
PART TWO — The Nature of Source   15
PART THREE — The Key to Enlightenment   29
PART FOUR — Living from Source   39
PART FIVE — The Source Ladder   45

Closing — The Ladder Continues   51
Glossary   53
About the Author   55

BOOK COVER — ABOUT THE CRYSTAL

The crystal on the cover is not decoration.

It is part of the transmission.

Its structure, clarity, and vertical form hold a precise movement of Source energy — the same frequency that threads through the book itself. This crystal was chosen because it resonates with the core intention of The Source Ladder: remembrance, alignment, and the quiet return to what is already true.

Crystals express energy through form.

Books express energy through language.

Here, the two work together.

The frequency of this crystal supports the frequency of the text. It amplifies the movement of awareness the book is designed to open. Its presence on the cover is a visual anchor — a simple, direct way to attune the reader before the first page is even turned.

This crystal stands as a symbol of clarity, verticality, and connection.

It contributes to the field of the book, and the book contributes to the field of the crystal.

Both carry the same Source movement.

This is why it belongs here.

PREFACE

Why write this book?

And what do I hope it will add to the human collective?

I've asked myself these questions many times. I've been on a spiritual path for more than forty-five years, reading, studying, and absorbing the teachings of spiritual masters and some of the most brilliant minds on the planet. Their insights have shaped me, challenged me, and opened doors I didn't know existed.

But this book isn't about religion, or any particular philosophy, or the teachings of any one individual. It's not meant to point people toward a lineage, a doctrine, or a belief system. What I've come to understand is that the Key to Enlightenment is absurdly simple — so simple it can be stated in three words. The challenge is understanding them.

If you were shown Einstein's equation for the theory of relativity without the supporting explanation, it would be meaningless. In the same way, if I gave you the Key to Enlightenment in three words, most readers would not fully comprehend it — and it would make for a very short book. Individuals have spent years, even lifetimes, seeking the answers to existence. What I offer here is the answer, along with the supporting understanding that makes it recognizable.

You do not need to read hundreds of books, study the teachings of masters, or dedicate your life to meditation and prayer to awaken. The answers are already within you. This book is written for those who have not yet encountered the teachers, teachings, or experiences that reveal what has always been present.

My intention is to share my understanding of existence, shaped by decades of seeking, questioning, and direct experience. I'm writing for the seekers — the people who feel that quiet pull toward something deeper, something truer, something they can't quite name but cannot ignore. I'm not trying to convert or convince. I'm simply offering what I've learned, in the hope it helps someone recognize what has always lived within them.

INTRODUCTION

Every seeker begins with a question they cannot ignore. It may appear as restlessness, a sense that something essential is missing, or a quiet awareness that life is more than the surface of our daily routines. Once that question arises, it changes how we see everything. This book is for anyone who feels that pull. You don't need a spiritual background, a belief system, or a specific practice. The seeker's path is not about becoming something new. It is about recognizing what has always been present.

Throughout this book, I use the word **Source** to describe the deeper intelligence behind existence. Some call it God, Consciousness, the Self, the Divine, the Void, or the Quantum Field. The name doesn't matter. What matters is understanding that Source is not separate from you. It is the awareness behind your thoughts, the stillness beneath your emotions, and the quiet guidance that has shaped your life in ways you may not have noticed.

The purpose of this book is simple: to help you recognize that connection for yourself.

Part One shares the arc of my own journey — not as a template, but as an example of how Source moves through a human life. Your path may look nothing like mine. It doesn't need to. What matters is learning to see the thread of guidance in your own experience.

The chapters that follow explore the nature of Source, the structure of consciousness, and how to align with what is already true. These ideas are not meant to be adopted as beliefs. They are meant to be tested and recognized within your own awareness.

You don't need to change your life to understand Source.
You don't need to seek enlightenment or become someone different.
You only need to notice what has always been here.

This Introduction opens the door.

In Part One you will begin to walk through it.

PART ONE — The Nature of the Seeker

A seeker is not a special kind of person. A seeker is simply someone who feels — often without knowing why — that there is something more to life than what appears on the surface. This feeling can arise as longing, curiosity, restlessness, or a quiet sense that something essential is missing. It may appear suddenly or grow slowly over years, but once it awakens, it becomes the subtle compass of a person's life.

The seeker's path is rarely linear. It moves in cycles: periods of clarity followed by periods of forgetting, moments of deep connection followed by stretches of ordinary life. These cycles are not mistakes or failures. They are part of the natural rhythm of awakening. Forgetting creates the space for deeper remembering. Stillness prepares the ground for insight. Even confusion has its place, softening the structures that keep us separate from what is true.

What distinguishes a seeker is not belief, discipline, or spiritual knowledge. It is the simple fact that the longing does not go away. Even when life becomes busy, even when responsibilities take over, even when the path seems to disappear, the longing remains quietly alive. It may dim, but it never extinguishes. It waits.

This longing is not a flaw. It is not a sign of incompleteness. It is the movement of Source within you — the pull of your own deeper nature calling you home. The seeker is not searching for something outside themselves. They are being drawn toward what they already are.

Every seeker experience guidance, though it may not be recognized at the time. It can appear as synchronicity, intuition, unexpected opportunities, or the sudden appearance of a teacher or book at exactly the right moment. It can also appear through challenges, endings, or the collapse of old structures. Guidance does not always feel gentle, but it is always precise.

The seeker's life is shaped by this invisible movement. Even when they believe they are lost, they are being carried. Even when they feel disconnected, the connection is still present. The seeker's journey is not about becoming spiritual. It is about recognizing the presence that has been with them from the beginning.

The longing is the first sign.
The guidance is the second.
The recognition is the third.

Together, they form the arc of awakening.

The Longing to Awaken

Awakening is what seekers yearn for. It is what I yearned for. It is a longing that lives beneath everything else, an ache that never fully disappears. If you are reading this book, I believe you feel it too.

There came a point in my life when nothing else mattered but this yearning. I still lived a normal human life — relationships, work, responsibilities — but once the spark of seeking was lit, that life felt like a façade. I imagined living in seclusion on a mountain, or disappearing into an ashram in India, or stepping away from the noise of humanity altogether.

These may not be your experiences; we are each unique. But once you become a seeker, something shifts. The world you knew begins to fade.

A seeker is not someone who chooses a spiritual path. A seeker is someone for whom the path becomes unavoidable. It begins quietly — an inner pull, a sense that something deeper is moving beneath the surface of ordinary life. You may not understand it at first. You simply know you can't ignore it.

My own path unfolded this way. Not through dramatic revelation, but through a series of precise movements that only made sense in hindsight.

Assignment to Alaska

Before any of this, I served with the Air Force's Hurricane Hunters.

I loved the work and the sense of purpose it gave me. But when I received an isolated assignment to Shemya, Alaska, everything shifted. My wife and children moved to England to be near her family, and I found myself facing uncertainty on every front. Before leaving for Alaska, we visited family in California. My uncle, a devotee of Paramahansa Yogananda,[1] listened as I told him I felt ready for some kind of change. I also told him I had three things I needed to sell — a car, an antique desk, and a house. Leaving all of that behind was a financial concern, and I had no idea how it would work out.

He said something simple: "It's okay to ask God for help." I had nothing to lose, so I prayed.

The next day, my brother called and offered to buy the antique desk. The day after that, a woman answered the ad for my car. She said her husband wasn't well and she had been praying for a car exactly like mine. One week after arriving in Alaska, a contract arrived for the sale of the house.

It was my first clear sign that prayers had meaning. It was hard to ignore the series of events.

The Path Begins

Before I left for Alaska, my uncle handed me *Autobiography of a Yogi*[2]. I read it while stationed there and was drawn to the idea of Enlightened Beings. The book mentioned the *Bhagavad Gita*[3] and

---

1 Paramahansa Yogananda (1893–1952) was a spiritual teacher whose book *Autobiography of a Yogi* introduced many Western readers to meditation and yogic philosophy.

2 *Autobiography of a Yogi* is Yogananda's spiritual classic, widely known for its accounts of yogic masters and its influence on Western seekers.

3 The *Bhagavad Gita* is a foundational text of Indian philosophy exploring duty, devotion, and the nature of the Self.

I remember telling a coworker I hoped to read it someday, though I had no idea how that would happen on a remote island.

We lived in an eight-room Quonset hut with a small dayroom. When I mentioned the Gita, my friend asked, "What's the name of the book?" I told him, and he walked to his room and returned with a copy. He said he had picked it up in a used bookstore in New York while waiting for his flight to Alaska. He never opened it and didn't know why he bought it.

Moments like this began forming a pattern.

Assigned to Nebraska

After Alaska, I was assigned to a base in Nebraska. A coworker introduced me to her friend who was visiting from New Jersey. He told me there was an Enlightened Being in upstate New York. He believed this person was "the real thing," and urged me to go see him because there were only a few remaining three-day retreats before he returned to India. I felt compelled to go.

I didn't know until I arrived that the teacher was Swami Muktananda, Guru of the Siddha Yoga lineage[4]. The atmosphere was focused, disciplined, and charged with purpose. At one point, the singer Roberta Flack — who was attending — sang a few songs for Baba. It was a beautiful, unexpected moment that added to the sense that something extraordinary was unfolding.

I loved it.

Something shifted during that intensive. Not outwardly, but inwardly. A recognition. A sense of alignment. A quiet certainty that I had stepped into something real.

---

4 Siddha Yoga is a lineagebased meditation tradition rooted in the teachings of Swami Muktananda and his Guru, Bhagavan Nityananda.

Before leaving the ashram, we were told there was a directory of spiritual centers throughout the world. I searched the Siddha Yoga directory.

There was only one center in the entire state of Nebraska.

It was in another town, but only four minutes from my home.

I attended weekly gatherings. The teachings resonated deeply, and the sense of recognition grew.

Retired from the Military

Sixteen months later, the pull became strong enough that I retired from the military without a plan. I had no job lined up and no clear sense of what would come next. I placed all my trust in Divine Will. I returned to New York to live in the Siddha Yoga community. My intention was simple: to go wherever I needed to go to be in alignment with the Divine.

I let go of everything — my career, my former life, and the identity I had built. We sold our home, and my wife and children moved into a rental. It was a time of uncertainty, but also a time of clarity. I felt guided, even though I didn't know where the guidance was leading.

After three weeks in the ashram, it became clear that I wasn't meant to stay in the community.

Then the phone rang.

The Call and the Redirection

It was my wife. A company had phoned the house looking for me.

A former Air Force acquaintance who lived near us woke my wife at six in the morning asking for a copy of my résumé — one I had written but never sent. He took it to his own interview and handed it to the person who later called my wife.

I returned the call and spoke to a recruiter from an aerospace corporation. We scheduled an interview. In that moment, I understood: I wasn't meant to abandon my life. I was being redirected.

I was hired as a Senior Engineer. Only later did I understand the significance. Six months earlier, at a coworker's retirement party, he had announced he'd been hired as a Senior Engineer at an aerospace company. We barely knew each other, yet at the end of his speech he turned, locked eyes with me, and said, "This could happen to you too." At the time it made no sense. But with the job offer in hand, the moment returned with perfect clarity. Guidance often looks like coincidence until you see the pattern.

Colorado, Divorce, and the Transfer to California

After accepting the engineering position, we moved to Colorado. Before that move, Swami Muktananda transitioned, and the lineage was passed to his protégé and translator, Malti, who became Gurumayi Chidvilasananda. I continued attending Siddha Yoga events whenever possible. While living in Colorado, I attended two satsangs with Gurumayi — one in New Mexico and one in Los Angeles. Each time, the same feeling returned: recognition, and alignment.

These were not dramatic experiences. They were steady confirmations that the thread was still guiding me.

Life settled into a new rhythm, but the inner pull toward the Divine never left. Over time, my marriage began to fracture. The separation was painful, but it unfolded with a strange clarity, as though something larger was guiding the process.

Eventually, we divorced. Our children remained with my wife.

My life as an engineer continued. I was promoted, transferred to California, and given new responsibilities. On the surface, everything looked successful. But beneath it all, the seeker in me was not gone— only quiet.

Two months before the move, something unusual began happening: I started seeing the number 11:11 everywhere. A friend even commented on how often it appeared when we were together.

When I arrived in California, I leased a temporary mailbox. The address was 1111 El Camino. That made me smile. Over the years I lived there, the pattern continued—111, 222, 333, 444, 555, 12:12. My cleaner's bill once came to $11.11. There were too many moments to list, but each one felt like a quiet nudge, a reminder that something larger was at work.

Guidance rarely announces itself.

It simply moves you.

Meeting Judi and the Return of Synchronicity

Then I met Judi.

From the moment we crossed paths, synchronicity returned. We were married in less than a year. On our first date, she said, "I'm on the spiritual path." She expected that to scare me off. Instead, it felt like a door reopening.

Although we came from different traditions, we soon found a spiritual community we both loved — one that honored both Jesus Christ and the lineage of Paramahansa Yogananda. I reread *Autobiography of a Yogi* and felt a renewed connection to Sri Anandamayi Ma[5]— an Enlightened Being who arrived on this planet already merged with the Divine. I found myself drawn once again to the teachings that had shaped my earlier awakening.

---

5 Sri Anandamayi Ma (1896–1982) was a revered Indian saint known for her spontaneous realization of the Divine and her profound presence.

Judi and I attended two satsangs with Gurumayi in San Francisco. These gatherings deepened the sense that the thread of my path had never left — it had simply evolved.

My life during those years was full of synchronicities. I didn't always understand them, but I felt guided. I felt protected. And I was deeply grateful for the grace that seemed to follow me.

Retiring Again, a New Job, and India

All of this — the synchronicities, the teachers, the communities — reopened the door. The longing returned, stronger than before. Once again, I felt my spiritual path was more important than my job. And once again, I retired without a plan.

I retired from aerospace. I wasn't financially adept, so I soon found myself needing work. But even this became part of the unfolding. I accepted a position with a software company, and after a year, they sent me to India on business. I was able to bring Judi with me.

After completing my assignment, we had a few days to explore. The company arranged a driver, and we asked him to take us to holy sites — though we had no idea where that would lead. We traveled to Rishikesh, on the Ganges, and to Haridwar. Then, without any planning on our part, the driver took us to a beautiful white marble ashram.

When I stepped inside, I realized where we were: the resting place of Sri Anandamayi Ma.

Source Revealed

When I stepped into the white marble ashram and realized where I was, I felt only awe. It was quiet, immediate, and beyond thought. I didn't fully understand the significance of what had happened. I only knew I was standing in a place I had never planned to visit, yet had somehow been guided to without a single conscious decision.

It wasn't until much later, after returning home, that the full weight of the moment reached me. I realized how impossible it was to have arrived there by chance. I saw the thread that had been pulling me for years — through teachers, synchronicities, detours, and returns — all leading to this one moment of recognition.

And when that understanding came, it overwhelmed me. With gratitude, with the unmistakable knowing that I have been blessed, guided, and protected all my life. This was a moment of awakening.

A Call to Share What I Had Learned

Nineteen years later, my time in California came to an end when my wife transitioned. A year after her passing, I moved to Colorado to begin a new chapter. Once I settled, the weight of the loss settled with me, and I found myself wondering what would come next. Throughout my life, I had occasional readings with psychics, intuitives, and a medium. I did not depend on them, but I found their insights interesting, and sometimes they aligned with things I was already sensing. After such a major change in my life, I felt it was appropriate to seek guidance.

I had read a book by Maureen J. St. Germain, an internationally recognized teacher and intuitive. I decided to schedule an Akashic Records reading with her. The Akashic Records are often described as "Books of Life," said to contain the history of a soul across lifetimes.

My question for the session was simple:

"Have I accomplished my purpose for this life, and am I done?"

To my surprise, Maureen said the Akashic Wisdom Keepers were laughing. She told me that while I had accomplished much of my purpose, I was only just beginning. I was to share my knowledge of Source before returning.

I was in my seventies at the time, and I was skeptical. I asked how I was supposed to do such a thing. The response was direct:

"Write a book. Go on social media. Figure it out."

Part of our soul growth requires us to show up, make choices, and awaken. Being told exactly how to accomplish the task would have been like being handed the answers to a test before taking it. The point was not to be given a plan — the point was to step forward. With great respect for Maureen's reading, it gave me pause. After the reading, I had no idea how to proceed. Writing a book felt unrealistic, and I had very little experience with social media. While I was pondering her message, I found myself wanting a second perspective — not out of doubt, but to understand whether I truly still had work to do.

The Confirmation of My Purpose

I belonged to a spiritual group that met online once a month. Three or four months after my reading with Maureen, I learned one of the members of my spiritual group was an Akashic Records reader. I hesitated to ask her for a reading because we were fellow members of the group, and I didn't want to take advantage of that connection.

But I was feeling lost in several ways, so I reached out and asked if she would be willing to do a reading, and that I would gladly pay her fee. Her name is Ceree Eberly, and she is remarkable. She accessed my Records and confirmed everything Maureen had told me.

Ceree provided a transcript of the reading, which allows me to share some of what was said.

When I asked about my soul's purpose and whether I had completed it, the reply was:

"Oh, we would say the work has just gotten started."

Later in the reading, they said:

"Your focus is not the physical body — it is the soul you are gifted at healing." And:

"You have been a sage to advise and counsel those on the journey of the soul."

In a later reading, they added:

"We like the theme of 'enlightenment coach,' as it can imply both spiritual, emotional, and physical enlightenment and healing." What those readings gave me was something I hadn't felt since my wife passed: purpose. I wasn't suicidal, but I was drifting. I had withdrawn from the world, unsure why I was still here or what remained for me to do. When both Maureen and Ceree independently told me that my work was not finished — that Source expected me to stay, to share what I understood about existence — something in me reawakened. Their readings didn't give me a mission; they reminded me that I still had one.

These messages clarified something I had sensed for years but had never fully acknowledged.

Source had been with me all along.

Not as an idea.
Not as a belief.
As the underlying reality of my life.

Nothing had been wasted.
Nothing had been wrong.
Nothing had been out of place.

The path was never about becoming spiritual.

It was about recognizing what had always been present.

The longing that had driven me for decades was not a search for something outside myself. It was the pull of Source calling me back to what had always been true. The teachers I met were expressions of that same Source. The synchronicities were its language. The detours were its way of shaping me. The moments of forgetting were part of the remembering.

And in that recognition, the seeker in me finally understood:

Source is not something you find.
Source is what you are.

The Return to the Reader

Looking back over the arc of my life, I can see now that the seeker's path is not a straight line. It rises and falls. It disappears and returns. It pulls us forward, then leaves us standing still until we are ready for the next step.

For years, I believed I was searching for something outside myself — a teacher, a community, a place, a moment of clarity. But every step, even the ones that felt like detours, was leading me toward a single realization:

Source was never separate from me.

And the same is true for you.

Your path may look nothing like mine. You may never travel to India, or sit with a teacher, or experience synchronicities that rearrange your life. You may not feel a dramatic longing or a sudden awakening.

But the form of the path is not what matters.

What matters is the quiet truth beneath it:

Source is already present in your life, moving through every moment, every choice, every breath.

You don't need to seek it in the way I did.
You don't need to leave your life or abandon anything.

You don't need to become spiritual.
You don't need to believe anything new.

You only need to recognize what has always been true.

My story is not meant to be followed.

It is meant to be a mirror — a reminder that the same Presence that guided me is guiding you, in your own way, in your own timing, through the circumstances of your own life.

The path to Source is not a journey outward.

It is a remembering inward.

And so here I am — aware of my knowing, and here to share Oneness with you, the seeker.

I am doing exactly what the Wisdom Keepers told me to do.

Writing a book.

PART TWO — The Nature of Source

Source is the underlying reality of everything that exists — the intelligence behind life, the awareness within every being, and the stillness beneath every thought. Source is not separate from you. It is the essence of who you are.

Most people experience life as if they are separate from the Divine, separate from others, and separate from the world around them. This sense of separation is the root of suffering. But separation is an appearance, not a truth. The truth is Oneness. Everything arises from the same field of consciousness. Rumi (1207–1273), the Persian poet and Sufi mystic, wrote: "As long as you believe in God, you remain separate, and fear survives."

Source is not something you believe in. It is something you recognize.

This recognition does not come through effort or study. It comes through a shift in perception — a moment when the mind becomes quiet enough for you to notice what has always been present. The seeker's longing is not a desire for something new. It is the pull of your own deeper nature calling you back to itself.

Source expresses itself through guidance, synchronicity, intuition, and the quiet movements that shape a life. These movements are not random. They are precise. When you look back, you can see the moments that redirected you, protected you, or opened a door you didn't know existed.

Source is not dramatic. It is exact.

It does not shout. It reveals.

Every seeker experiences this recognition in their own way. For some, it appears as a sudden awakening. For others, it unfolds slowly over years.

To understand Source is to understand your own nature.

To recognize Source is to recognize that you are not separate from anything.

To live from Source is to live from clarity, humility, and alignment.

Source is not a concept.

It is the ground of Being — the quiet presence that has been with you since the beginning, the intelligence that guided your life long before you knew how to listen, the truth that remains when everything else falls away.

The seeker longs for Source.

But the deeper truth is that Source has always been longing for you — waiting for the moment you become still enough to notice what has never been absent.

What Source Is Not

Source is not a deity watching from above. It is not a Being with preferences, judgments, or conditions. It does not reward or punish. It does not keep score. These ideas come from human psychology, not from the nature of the Divine.

Source is not separate from you.

It is not something you reach, earn, or ascend toward.

It is the awareness already present within you — the ground of your existence.

Source is not the mind.

The mind interprets, analyzes, and reacts.

Source simply is.

The mind moves.

Source remains.

Source is not emotion.

Emotions rise and fall. They are temporary states shaped by memory, conditioning, and circumstance. Source is the stillness beneath those movements — the presence that notices them.

Source is not intuition, though intuition can reflect it.

Intuition is a movement within the human system.

Source is the field from which all movements arise.

Source is not energy in the way people often describe it.

Energy fluctuates.

Source does not.

Energy expresses.

Source is the foundation that allows expression.

Source is not a path, a lineage, or a tradition.

Paths are ways of remembering.

Source is what is remembered.

Source is not an experience.

Experiences come and go.

Even profound spiritual experiences fade.

Source is the awareness in which all experiences appear.

Source is not something you visit in meditation.

It is not a state you enter.

It is the presence that remains when all states dissolve.

Source is not distant.

It is not hidden.

It is not waiting for you to become worthy.

It is the quiet truth behind every moment of your life — the intelligence that guided you long before you knew how to listen When you remove what Source is not, what remains is simple:
Source is the awareness reading these words.
It is the presence behind your thoughts.
It is the life moving through your body.
It is the intelligence shaping your path.
It is the essence of who you are.

You do not find Source.

You recognize it.

And that recognition becomes possible only when the false ideas fall away.

How Source Moves Through a Life

Source does not move through life the way people imagine. It moves from within — as intuition, timing, synchronicity, and the quiet shifts that redirect a life without force.

Most people overlook this because they expect guidance to be dramatic. They expect a sign, a revelation, or a moment that feels unmistakably divine. But Source rarely works that way. Its movements are subtle, precise, and often only visible in hindsight.

Source moves through a life by arranging the right people, the right circumstances, and the right openings at the exact moment they are needed. It is not random. It is not accidental. It is the intelligence of the universe expressing itself through the details of your life.

Sometimes Source moves by opening a door.

Sometimes it moves by closing one.

Sometimes it moves by placing you somewhere you never planned to be.

Guidance is not always comfortable. It can appear as loss, change, or the collapse of something you thought was essential. But even these moments carry precision. They clear the space for what must come next.

Source moves through a life the way a river shapes a landscape — quietly, consistently, and with a direction that becomes obvious only when you step back and see the whole picture.

You do not have to understand the movement for it to be happening.

You do not have to believe in it for it to be true.

You only have to become still enough to notice what has always been guiding you.

When you look back at your life, you can see the moments that made no sense at the time but were necessary for your growth, your awakening, and your return to your own deeper nature.

This is how Source moves.

Not with noise, but with precision.

Not with force, but with alignment.

Not from outside, but from within.

Source is not seeking anything. It is simply expressing itself through form, the way light naturally radiates or water naturally flows. When we awaken, it is not because Source has decided to know itself more fully; it is because the human system has become clear enough to recognize what has always been true. Awakening is not Source discovering itself — it is you discovering that you were never separate from it.

The Mechanics of Alignment

Alignment is not something you create. It is something you notice.

Source is always moving, always guiding, always present. The question is whether you are quiet enough, honest enough, and willing enough to recognize that movement. Most people try to align with life by controlling it. They plan, push, analyze, and force outcomes. But alignment is not control. Alignment is cooperation with a deeper intelligence that already knows the next step.

Alignment begins with stillness — not the absence of activity, but the absence of inner noise.

When the mind settles, even briefly, you can feel the difference between a movement that is yours alone and a movement that comes from Source.

A movement from ego feels tight, urgent, or fueled by fear.

A movement from Source feels clear, steady, and unforced.

This distinction is subtle at first, but it becomes unmistakable over time.

Alignment also shows itself through resonance.

When something is aligned, it carries a quiet "yes" that does not need justification.

When something is misaligned, it carries a subtle resistance — a heaviness, a hesitation, or a sense that you are pushing against the grain of your own life.

You learn to trust these signals.

You learn to recognize the difference between effort and flow.

Synchronicity increases when alignment is present.

Doors open without strain.

The right people appear.

The timing becomes precise.

You find yourself in the exact place you need to be without having planned it.

This is not magic.

It is the natural movement of Source when you stop interfering.

Alignment is not passive. It requires honesty, humility, and the willingness to let go of what no longer fits. Sometimes alignment asks you to step forward. Sometimes it asks you to wait. Sometimes it asks you to release something you once held tightly.

The mechanics are simple:

Stillness — so you can hear.
Discernment — so you can tell the difference.
Willingness — so you can follow the movement.
Trust — so you don't collapse back into fear.

Alignment is not about perfection.

It is about listening.

When you live from alignment, life becomes less about effort and more about recognition. You begin to see that the same intelligence that guided you in the past is guiding you now. You begin to feel the thread moving through your life in real time, not just in hindsight.

This is the beginning of living from Source rather than from separation.

What If I'm Wrong?

Every sincere seeker eventually reaches this question.

I did too.

How do I know this is true?

How do I know there aren't more fields, or fewer?

How do I know there isn't a dark realm, or another light realm, or a structure of existence I haven't seen?

The honest answer is simple:

I don't.

And I don't need to.

This book is not a map of the universe.

It is a reflection of awareness.

It does not claim to describe every realm, every dimension, or every possibility.

It points to something far more intimate and far more reliable: the experience of being aware.

You cannot prove Oneness.
You cannot disprove it.
You can only recognize it.

Every tradition that has ever spoken of the Divine — from the ancient sages to modern mystics — has pointed to the same truth in different language:

Only awareness is constant.
Only consciousness is undeniable.
Only the sense of "I exist" remains when everything else falls away.

As a brilliant doctor once said,

"No one is going to convince you that you don't exist." That is the foundation.

Science, in its own way, is beginning to gesture toward the same mystery. Some findings suggest consciousness may not arise from the brain alone. Near-death research hints that death may be a transition rather than a disappearance.

Physics reminds us that energy is never lost.

And certain scientific models treat awareness as a basic feature of reality, not a byproduct of the brain.

But even these are not proofs.

They are resonances.

In the end, every seeker stands in the same place:

You believe what you recognize.
You trust what you experience.
You follow what feels true in your own awareness.

If there are other realms, other fields, other expressions of existence, they would still arise within the same Source.

If there is darkness, it exists within the same Light.

If there are infinite nested realities, they unfold within the same awareness reading these words.

This book does not ask you to accept a cosmology.

It invites you to look at the one thing you cannot deny:

You are aware.

Everything else — every belief, every teaching, every possibility — arises within that awareness. And that is enough.

The Movement from Mind to Awareness

The mind and awareness are not two different things. They are two expressions of the same Source. Thought is not separate from the one who thinks it. Awareness is not separate from the thoughts it notices. All of it arises from the same field of consciousness.

The movement from mind to awareness is not a movement from one place to another. It is the recognition that both are expressions of the same Source. What changes is not what you are — what changes is what you believe yourself to be.

Most people live as if the mind is the Self. They identify with thoughts, emotions, and interpretations. But the mind is simply one way Source expresses itself. Awareness is another. Neither is higher or lower. Neither is more spiritual. Both are movements within the same field.

When you recognize this, something subtle shifts.

You stop treating thoughts as personal.
You stop treating awareness as a special state.
You begin to see that everything arising within you — every thought, every emotion, every moment of clarity or confusion — is Source appearing as this experience.

There is no separation.

There is no observer over here and thoughts over there.

There is only Source, expressing as both.

This recognition brings a quiet freedom.

Not because the mind disappears, but because you no longer mistake its movements for something separate from your true nature. You see thought as a wave in the ocean of consciousness — not separate from the ocean, not outside of it, not other than it.

Awareness is the ocean.
Thought is the wave.
Both are water.

The movement from mind to awareness is the moment you recognize the water.

You do not silence the mind.
You do not escape thought.
You do not rise above anything.

You simply see that everything arising within you is the same Source expressing in different forms.

This recognition dissolves the struggle.

You no longer fight the mind or chase awareness.
You no longer divide your inner experience into "spiritual" and "not spiritual."
You no longer imagine that awakening requires you to become something other than what you already are.

The mind moves.
Awareness notices.
Both are Source.

When this is seen, the seeker relaxes.

The effort falls away.
The sense of separation begins to dissipate.
And you begin to live from a deeper truth — not as someone trying to awaken, but as the Source expressing itself through a human life.

This is the threshold of recognition.

The Threshold of Recognition

Recognition does not arrive as an event. It arrives as a shift — a quiet, unmistakable seeing that what you have been searching for has been present all along. It is not dramatic. It is not emotional. It is not an experience you enter and leave. It is the moment the illusion of separation begins to dissolve.

Up to this point, the seeker believes they are moving toward something — progressing, learning, refining, awakening. But the truth is simpler: the seeker is being carried toward a recognition that has nothing to do with effort.

The threshold is reached when you begin to sense that everything arising within you — every thought, every emotion, every moment of clarity or confusion — is not separate from the Source you have been seeking. You begin to see that the mind is not an obstacle, and awareness is not a destination. Both are expressions of the same field.

This is the moment when the seeker stops trying to awaken and begins to notice what has always been awake.

The threshold is not a place you arrive at.

It is a veil that becomes thin.
It is the softening of the belief that you are separate from the life moving through you.

You begin to see that guidance was never external.
Synchronicity was never coincidence.
Intuition was never a message from somewhere else.

It was all Source, expressing as your life.

The threshold is the recognition that nothing has ever been outside of Source — not your thoughts, not your choices, not your mistakes, not your path. Everything has been part of the same movement.

At this point, the seeker begins to be more aligned.

The struggle loses its meaning.
The search loses its urgency.
The mind loses its authority.

What remains is a quiet readiness — a sense that something true is about to reveal itself, not because you have earned it, but because you have finally stopped resisting it.

This is the threshold.

It is the final moment before the recognition that changes everything.

It is the doorway to the Key to Enlightenment.

PART THREE — The Key to Enlightenment

The Questions at the Heart of the Journey

What is Source?
What is Consciousness?
What is Awareness?
What is God?

Humanity has asked these questions for as long as we've been able to think. You may have asked them yourself. They seem mysterious, yet the truth behind them is simple. Recognizing that truth, however, can take a lifetime — or many lifetimes.

During my forty-five years of searching, the answers were shown to me again and again. I heard them, but I didn't fully understand them. As a seeker, you may have heard these answers as well, yet still find yourself searching. That is part of the journey.

When you awaken to Source, something shifts.

Your reality changes.

The world does not look different — you do.

And this is where the Key to Enlightenment begins:

Only Source Exists.

These three words are the Key to Enlightenment promised to you.

Everything you see, everything you experience, everything you believe to be separate or external is an expression of the same Source field. You are not apart from it. You are not seeking it. You are remembering it.

What "Only Source Exists" Really Means

This is not a philosophy.

It is a description of reality.

Source is the field of pure existence from which everything arises — the essence behind form, the intelligence behind life, the awareness behind your awareness. Every person, every object, every thought, every moment is an expression of that same field. Nothing is outside of it.

When you recognize this — not as an idea, but as a lived truth — your relationship with reality changes. You stop searching for something "out there" and begin remembering what has always been within you.

To understand how this truth expresses itself in your daily life, it helps to look at the three ways Source appears within your experience: as consciousness, as awareness, and as the sense of self.

Consciousness, Awareness, and the Self

If Only Source Exists, then everything you experience is happening within Source — including you.

Consciousness is Source expressing as the capacity to know.
Awareness is Source recognizing itself through you.
The Self is the temporary identity you inhabit while moving through this lifetime.

These are not separate things. They are different ways of describing the same underlying reality.

Consciousness is the light.
Awareness is the seeing.
The Self is the lens.
Source is the field behind them all.

If this is our true nature, the obvious question arises:

Why don't we experience life this way?

The answer is woven into the design of incarnation itself.

Why We Forget

If Only Source Exists, why don't we experience life that way?

Because forgetting is part of the design.

When you enter a lifetime, you take on an identity — a name, a history, a personality, a story. This identity becomes the lens through which you experience the world. It isn't a flaw or a mistake. It is how Source experiences itself from a unique point of view.

The illusion of separation allows you to explore, to learn, to grow, and ultimately to remember what you truly are.

Forgetting is the beginning of the journey.
Remembering is the return.

And even within the illusion of separation, something in you remembers.

That remembering begins quietly.

Awakening and remembering are not the same movement. Awakening is the moment of recognition — the sudden seeing of what has always been true. It can happen in an instant because it is a shift in perception, not a change in identity. Remembering, however, is the integration of that recognition into the human system. It unfolds gradually because the body, mind, and nervous system need time to reorganize around the truth that has been seen. Awakening is the spark. Remembering is the embodiment.

How Remembering Begins

Remembering does not happen all at once. It begins quietly.

Something in you starts to question the assumptions you once accepted without thought. You feel a subtle pull toward truth, even if you cannot name it. Moments of clarity appear — brief, fleeting, but unmistakable.

You begin to sense that there is more to you than the identity you have carried, more to life than the roles you play, more to existence than the physical world.

This is the beginning of awakening: the recognition that the separation you believed in was never real.

The Shift in Perception

As remembering deepens, you begin to sense Source not as a concept, but as the living presence within everything. The boundaries you once believed in feel less solid. The world becomes more fluid, more connected, more alive.

You notice synchronicities that once seemed random.

You feel moments of peace that have no external cause.

You recognize that the awareness looking out through your eyes is the same awareness that animates all of existence. This shift is quiet, steady, and profoundly intimate.

The Dissolution of Separation

As this new way of seeing deepens, the sense of separation that once felt so real begins to change. You notice that the "you" who is aware and the "world" you are aware of are not as divided as you once believed.

The boundary between inner and outer becomes thinner.

Connection becomes natural. Presence becomes effortless.

You begin to experience the truth directly:

the separation was never real.

THE FOUR MOVEMENTS OF AWAKENING

Awakening does not happen all at once. It unfolds through natural shifts in perception — gentle movements that reveal what has always been true. These movements are not steps or stages. They do not happen in order. They simply describe the ways consciousness opens.

1. STILLNESS — THE LOOSENING OF IDENTITY

Awakening begins when the inner noise quiets and you sense the presence beneath thought. Stillness is the moment the seeker relaxes, and the urgency of searching begins to fade.

Within this Movement, three Fields appear naturally. They describe the qualities of awareness that arise as identity loosens:

• **Stillness**

The quiet ground beneath all experience. Stillness reveals the presence that exists before thought, emotion, or identity.

• **Clarity**

The recognition that awareness is One. Clarity dissolves confusion and reveals the truth beneath appearances.

• **Alignment**

The sense of being internally congruent — thoughts, actions, and deeper knowing moving in the same direction.

2. ENERGY — THE RECOGNITION OF GUIDANCE

As Stillness deepens, you begin to notice the subtle movements within your experience — intuition, resonance, synchronicity. Life feels less random and more connected. You recognize that guidance is not something outside you. It is the movement of Source within you.

Within this Movement, three Fields express the living intelligence of awareness:

• Flow

Life unfolding with ease and precision. Flow is the movement of Source through your experience without resistance.

• Presence

Full contact with the moment as it is. Presence is awareness resting in itself, unfiltered and unforced.

• Connection

The felt sense that nothing is separate. Connection reveals the relational nature of consciousness — everything touching everything.

3. CLARITY — THE DISSOLUTION OF SEPARATION

Clarity is the recognition that the awareness within you is the same awareness in all things. The boundary between "inner" and "outer" softens. Everything becomes transparent to its Source.

Within this Movement, three Fields illuminate the transparency of experience:

• Expansion

The widening of perception. Expansion opens the sense of self beyond personal identity into a larger field of awareness.

• Power

Not force, but the natural strength of truth. Power is the stability and confidence that arise when you live from what is real.

- **Radiance**

The natural luminosity of awareness. Radiance is the effortless expression of truth through your presence.

4. ASCENSION — THE EMBODIMENT OF TRUTH

Ascension is not rising above life. It is living from truth within life. The mind reorganizes. The nervous system settles. You no longer experience yourself as a seeker, but as the expression of Source moving through a human life.

Within this Movement, three Fields anchor the embodiment of awakening:

- **Integration**

The weaving together of insight and embodiment. Integration is truth settling into the nervous system and daily life.

- **Return**

The movement back to Source after every experience. Return is the recognition that all paths lead inward.

- **Origin**

The recognition of the Source within you — the beginning and end of all experience, appearing as this moment.

THE MOVEMENTS AND FIELDS TOGETHER

Each Movement describes a broad shift in awakening.
Each Field describes a specific quality within that shift.

Together, they offer a simple, intuitive way of naming what is already unfolding within you.

Awakening is not an idea. It is a lived experience.

The Movements and Fields simply describe how consciousness opens within you, but they are not the point.
The point is how this opening expresses itself in your life.

Once you recognize the qualities of awakening within your own experience, the question becomes simple:

How do I live from this?

That is the movement into the next part of this book
— not the theory of awakening,
but the lived expression of it.

PART FOUR — Living From Source

The Rhythm of Remembering

Living from Source is not a constant state.

It is a rhythm — a movement of remembering and forgetting, opening and closing, clarity and confusion. This rhythm is not a flaw in your spiritual life. It is your spiritual life.

Forgetting is part of the design.

It allows you to rediscover what is true with deeper clarity each time. It softens the structures that keep you separate.

It prepares you for the next opening.

Remembering is not something you force.

It arrives quietly — in a moment of stillness, in a breath, in a feeling of peace that has no cause. It appears when you stop searching long enough to notice what has always been present.

Living from Source begins with recognizing this rhythm and trusting it.

You are not meant to hold perfect clarity at all times.

You are meant to awaken through the movement itself.

Living from Clarity

When you begin to recognize Source as the foundation of your life, something subtle shifts. You don't become a different person. You simply relate to life from a different frequency.

Challenges still arise, but they no longer define you.

Emotions still move through you, but they no longer consume you. Thoughts still appear, but they no longer feel like the whole truth.

Clarity is not the absence of difficulty.

It is the presence of awareness within difficulty.

Living from clarity means:

- responding instead of reacting

- listening instead of assuming

- allowing instead of resisting

- trusting instead of controlling

It means recognizing that every moment — even the uncomfortable ones — is part of the same movement of Source expressing itself through your life.

You don't need to maintain a spiritual state.

You only need to notice the presence that is already here.

The Human Path and the Divine Path

You are both human and divine.

Living from Source means honoring both.

Your humanity gives you texture, depth, and experience.
Your divinity gives you clarity, presence, and truth.

The human path is the path of learning.
The divine path is the path of remembering.

When you live from Source, these two paths merge.

You no longer see your humanity as an obstacle.
You see it as the very way Source experiences itself through you.

Your emotions, your relationships, your challenges, your joys — all of them are expressions of the same field of consciousness. Nothing is separate. Nothing is wasted. Nothing is outside the movement of awakening.

Living from Source does not remove you from life.
It brings you more fully into it.

The Return to the Reader

As you move through your own journey, you may not experience the same events I did. Your path will unfold in its own way, with its own timing, through the circumstances of your own life. But the essence is the same for all seekers:

Source is already present within you.

You don't need to search for it.

You don't need to earn it.

You don't need to become worthy of it.

You only need to recognize what has always been true.

Your life — every moment of it — is part of the movement of awakening.

The longing you feel is Source calling you home.

The guidance you receive is Source shaping your path.

The recognition you experience is Source remembering itself through you.

You are not separate from Source.

You never have been. You never will be.

Living from Source is not a destination.

It is a way of being — a quiet, steady remembrance of your own true nature.

And as you walk this path, know this:

You are guided.
You are supported.
You are held.
You are Source.

To understand how this recognition expresses itself across lifetimes and frequencies, we turn to the Source Ladder.

PART FIVE — The Source Ladder

The Source Ladder

The Source Ladder is a map of existence itself.

It points to something the human brain was never designed to fully comprehend: Source — the infinite, the One, the origin of all frequencies, all consciousness, all being.

The Source Ladder is not a vertical ascent.
It is a spiral of expanding recognition — rising through octaves while radiating outward in awareness, returning to Origin in every cycle.

Source has been given many names across cultures and ages:

God
Consciousness
The Void
The Absolute
Brahman
Tao
The Great Spirit
The One Mind

Even Christ expressed this truth when he said, "My Father and I are One."

Every tradition point to the same indivisible unity.

This book simply uses the word **Source** — the One behind all names.

The Source Ladder is the architecture of frequencies that make up all that exists. These frequencies are infinite, ranging from the densest expressions of matter to the most expanded realms of clarity and light. Everything you see, everything you feel, everything you are — is a frequency of Source.

Nikola Tesla once said, "If you want to find the secrets of the Universe, think in terms of energy, frequency and vibration."

You are a frequency of Source Energy — energy that has slowed, condensed, and lowered its vibration until it becomes matter. As Einstein said, "Matter is spirit reduced to the point of visibility." You are spirit made visible.

The Source Ladder is like the octaves of music. You begin at an entry frequency, and through experience, learning, and free will, you spiral through the octave of your lifetime. Each cycle expands your capacity for recognition. Some souls choose gentle paths. Others choose difficult lessons to spiral more rapidly through an octave of experience. All choices are honored.

When you complete one octave, you naturally expand into the next.

There is no beginning and no end to this movement.

You are immortal.

Death is not an ending — it is simply a shift to a clearer frequency band, a return to a less dense expression of the same consciousness.

The Source Ladder is the story of that movement.
It is the architecture of your existence.
It is the remembrance of who you truly are.

Enlightened vs. Awakened

A few rare individuals throughout history have lived in full awareness of Oneness. They did not believe in unity — they experienced it directly. Their sense of separation dissolved, and they lived from the recognition that all things arise from the same Source. These individuals are often called Enlightened — not because they reached a higher status, but because they remembered completely. Most of us live in a different state — a state of awakening.

Awakening is the recognition that something deeper exists. It is the sense that the world of form is not the whole story. It is the quiet knowing that you are more than your thoughts, your body, or your history. Awakening is the beginning of remembering, not the end.

The difference is simple:

Awakened means you sense the truth.
Enlightened means you live from it.

Neither is better.
Neither is required.
Both are natural expressions of consciousness moving through the spiral of the Source Ladder.

Awakening is not a lesser state — it is the doorway.
Enlightenment is not a reward — it is the full remembrance of what has always been true.

Every soul moves through these states in their own time.

There is no rush.
No competition.
No comparison.

Only the ongoing spiral — rising and expanding through the infinite octaves of the Source Ladder.

The Source Ladder and the Frequency Ladder describe the same territory from two different angles. The Source Ladder is the map — the structure of consciousness as it unfolds from Stillness to Origin. The Frequency Ladder is the movement through that map — the lived progression of recognition, embodiment, and integration. The Fields are the layers of the map, and the Movements are the shifts that occur as you pass through each layer. One describes the architecture. The other describes the experience.

The Source Frequencies

Everything in existence is an expression of Source, but it does not all express in the same way. Just as white light contains every color, Source contains every frequency — every quality, every movement, every form of consciousness.

A frequency is not a vibration you create.
It is a state of being you recognize.

Human beings experience these frequencies as qualities of consciousness — clarity, openness, compassion, courage, truth, stillness, presence. These qualities are not personal traits. They are expressions of the deeper reality within you.

When you feel peace, you are experiencing a frequency of Source. When you feel love, you are experiencing a frequency of Source. When you feel the pull toward truth, you are experiencing a frequency of Source.

Frequencies are not hierarchical.
They simply reflect different levels of clarity.

Some frequencies feel dense or contracted.
Others feel expansive or luminous.
But all of them arise from the same Source, and all of them lead back to it.

You do not need to force yourself into an expanded frequency.
You only need to notice the one you are in.

Every moment of your life is shaped by the frequency you are experiencing. When you are in fear, the world appears threatening. When you are in openness, the world appears spacious. When you are in clarity, the world appears simple.

The world does not change — your frequency does.

The Source Frequencies are the natural movements of consciousness returning to itself. They are the stepping stones of recognition, the subtle shifts that reveal the truth of your own nature. You have experienced them throughout your life, even if you did not have a name for them.

These frequencies form a natural progression — not a ladder to climb, but a map of how consciousness unfolds. This progression is what I call the Frequency Ladder. It is not a system to follow. It is a way of understanding the movements you have already lived.

The Source Frequencies are not something you achieve.
They are something you remember.

CLOSING — The Ladder Continues

This book began in Stillness because that is where every genuine shift begins.

Not with effort, not with striving, but with the simple willingness to stop and see what is already here. Stillness is the ground beneath every experience — the quiet that makes clarity possible.

From there, we moved into Energy — the movement of life within you.

Energy is not an obstacle to awakening; it is the material of awakening. When you stop resisting your inner experience, Energy becomes a guide rather than a threat. It shows you where you are holding on and where you are ready to let go.

Clarity emerges naturally when Stillness and Energy are no longer in conflict.

Clarity is not a reward for spiritual achievement. It is the natural state of perception when fear softens and identity loosens. In Clarity, you begin to see your experience without distortion, and the truth of your nature becomes unmistakably simple.

Ascension is the final movement — not upward, but inward.

It is the recognition that awareness is not something you create; it is what you are. Ascension is not an escape from the human experience, but a deeper participation in it, free from the weight of misunderstanding. It is the return to Source, not as a destination, but as your origin.

These four movements — Stillness, Energy, Clarity, and Ascension — are not steps to master.

They are dimensions of the same truth, each revealing a different aspect of what it means to be awake, present, and aligned.

If this book has offered anything, I hope it has shown that awakening is not distant or dramatic.

It is intimate.
It is ordinary.
It is already happening within you.

Thank you for walking this arc with me.

May Stillness steady you.
May Energy move freely through you.
May Clarity illuminate your path.
And may Ascension remind you of what you have always been.

Glossary

Ego / Identity

The collection of thoughts, memories, roles, and beliefs the mind uses to create a sense of "me." Identity is not destroyed in awakening — it simply loosens and becomes transparent.

Guidance

The natural intelligence of awareness expressing itself through intuition, resonance, clarity, and timing. Guidance is not external; it is the movement of Source within you.

Separation

The belief that you are a separate self, isolated from life. Awakening reveals that separation was never real — only a perception created by the mind.

Source

The origin of all experience — pure awareness, pure being, pure intelligence. Source is not elsewhere; it is the essence of what you are.

Transition

A movement from one state or form into another. Transition can refer to a shift in consciousness or, in a more personal sense, the passing from physical life into nonphysical existence.

Transparency

The recognition that all experience is made of awareness. Nothing is hidden. Nothing is separate. Everything is seen as an expression of the same Source.

ABOUT THE AUTHOR

Ronald J. Adams is a lifelong seeker, metaphysical philosopher, and spiritual system-builder whose work bridges lived experience with clear, grounded insight. For more than forty-five years, he has explored the nature of consciousness, the structure of awakening, and the quiet intelligence that moves through every human life.

His journey has taken him from military service to engineering, from spiritual communities to moments of profound synchronicity, and ultimately to the recognition that Only Source Exists. *The Source Ladder* emerged from decades of inquiry, direct experience, and the steady unfolding of remembrance.

Ronald writes for those who feel the subtle pull toward something deeper — the seekers, the intuitives, the ones who sense that life is more than the material world. His work is not about belief or doctrine. It is about clarity, recognition, and the lived experience of awakening.

He currently lives in Colorado, where he continues to refine his teachings, develop the Source Ladder system, and support others on their path of remembrance.

For more information go to   https://www.thesourceladder.com

www.ingramcontent.com/pod-product-compliance
Lightning Source LLC
Chambersburg PA
CBHW030859120726

48008CB00002B/54